Words
Of
Wisdom
Are
Words
To
Live
By

Published by Emerson Welch, Jr

Cover design by Emerson Welch, Jr

ISBN # 978-0-9704569-4-6

Dedicated to:
Emerson & Gloria Welch, my parents.

Thank you both for teaching me to always look at the glass as half full as oppose to seeing it as half empty. Providing me with that thought process was actually the embryo of why I see things the way I do now. I am an eternal optimist with a never say die state of mind because I had the privilege to witness how both of you have faced difficult challenges throughout my childhood and adult life. Although it may have appeared that I wasn't listening when either of you spoke, I actually was listening and learning. That is why I can truly say, ***"Words Of Wisdom Are Words To Live By".***

Thank You.

INTRODUCTION

"Words Of Wisdom Are Words To Live By" is a collection of poems and short compositions. The sole intent of this book is to provide motivation to think about things and circumstances we all face each day. While the book doesn't provide answers, it does a great job at making us understand that most of the answers many of us search for is within us all.

A Few Friends There

For all of us who've gone through something before
or are going through it now

Don't get fed up, just keep your head up; we'll get
through it some way, some how

Just be sure to stay persistent as you search for a
solution and you too shall prevail

Know that effort combined with a true belief in the
"Most High" and you'll never fail

These are just a few facts that poetically I decided
to share because I care

So when I reach the top of the ladder of success,
there'll be a few friends there.

A Gentle Shove

Change is good when things look destined to stay
the same
Progress requires it when familiar surroundings
seem strange
When the desire to leave overpowers the desire to
remain
That is when it is obvious that it is time for a
change

And so I look forward to the future and have
learned from the past.
If you choose to count me out, it means you're
terrible at math
My confidence from within comes from my belief
in the man above
I am on my way to a final destination called success
and your doubt in me is a gentle shove.

A Positive State Of Mind

When we spend time continuously crying and complaining about the past, it is a clear indication that we can't possibly be thinking about investing time in a positive state of mind; thereby lessening our chance of truly appreciating the present. By embracing a thought process that doesn't help us to become or remain positive, we are actually shortchanging our chances of succeeding in the future.

We must always control what we can control. Our positive state of mind should ALWAYS be within our control.

A Quality I Lack

Although some do their very best to try to stop me

I don't worry because I know the "Most High" has got me

So when people talk nonsense, I make an effort to get rid of them

Because friends til the end is something I'll never consider them

So I'm thinking, why waste time with people who really ain't saying a damn thing?

The truth is, I really don't have time to experience the drama they inevitably bring

So when a person feels the need to talk nonsense to me, they need to fall back

Because having a high tolerance for unproductive conversation is a quality I lack.

A Random Act Of Kindness

A random act of kindness trumps a wicked deed any day

So let's start the weekend off right by having something good to say

Let's reach out and touch someone who may have lost their way

Send an email, text or surprise them by calling and just saying, "hey"

You'd be surprised at the positive impact we can all have on someone else's day

All the negative nonsense is in the past and that's exactly where it should stay

Positive thoughts and actions is a part of my life's role I choose to play

I create my own destiny by always giving the best of me each and every day.

A Woman's Worth.....Does She Know It?

When a woman knows the value of her existence she is independently strong and is less likely to be hurt

And if we as men understood a woman's worth, we'd never hesitate to always put her first

We'd respect her not only for her obvious physical beauty but more importantly for the essence of her existence

Perhaps then we'd treat her as the treasure the "Most High" intended and we would do so with an unwavering persistence...........Always.

Words inspired by every woman I've ever met.

A Would Be Remorseful Shooter

I spit bars that are hard with the sole intent to make
souls repent
I don't claim to be righteous, I might just be bold
and in control when I choose to vent
I'm tired of hearing about of all the senseless
killing; because killing never makes sense
As a society, why are we so quick to shoot guns
instead of talking to another one when things get
tense
Does our conscience let us feel anything for the
innocent victim whose blood is now spilled and we
have now killed
And are we able to have any type of compassion for
the family that is in mourning this morning because
we didn't just chill
In addition to the gifts mom bought she always
taught me to consider what another person may be
feeling
Perhaps if I and many of us did this, we would all
witness a wounded society start a process called
healing
I mean if we had a child in this world whether it's a
boy or girl, we wouldn't want anyone to hurt it
With that thought in mind at this unfortunate time, I
must ask myself and other brothers, was it really
worth it???

Protect us all; PUT THE GUNS DOWN!!!

ALONE

When you sit in a room with someone who thinks
ONLY of him or her self, you may not feel lonely
but you are definitely ALONE.

Am I smart or do I think I know everything???

You ever notice how some people think you're smart when you help them figure something out but then think you're incredibly stupid when you mention the fact that you know exactly what their up to when they lie?

That's when they usually tell others, "He or she think they know everything" when they gossip about you.........SMDH

Another Sunday Morning

Another Sunday morning is what this thankful man
is blessed to see

I'll show my appreciation by trying to be the best
me I can possibly be

I'll continue to try and uplift others with the poetic
words I choose to write

So I'll have a feeling of personal satisfaction when I
bow my head to pray tonight

So as your eyes read these words that I've written,
please know you too are blessed

For you too have awaken to live yet another day
after what I hope was a good nights rest.

Answer The Call

Thank you lord for waking me up this morning in
the bed that you allowed me to lay

Please lord bless those too who are or have become
homeless here today

I asked that you provide for them just as you have
provided for me

Yes, I ask that you show them the way just as
you've always guided me

Help us all to understand that homelessness is an
issue that really affects us all

The phone I call compassion for humanity is steady
ringing; help us realize we need to answer the call.

As We Get Older

As we get older, we tend to see things for what they
are instead of just what we would like them to be

That vision enables us to make the necessary
adjustments to enhance the chance for us to
eventually succeed

The wisdom many of us acquire assists us with life
altering choices that must sometimes be made

Which means the pains from past decisions doesn't
remain, which ultimately enables them to fade

That's why we ought not dwell on the negative
disappointments and failures of the past.

Instead, we can focus on the opportunity to be
positive in the future and create memories that will
forever last.

A Positive mind is the foundation for positive effort

If positive poetry is a house of motivation,
I'm not on the outside; I go in
Though something's in life can be negative
at times, I write with a positive spin
And so my words are meant to encourage
others when circumstances seem hopeless
The primary reason I wrote this is simply to
inspire others to always stay focused.

Be Positive

Since we're blessed enough to live, why not be
positive?

Let's face it, negative energy is energy wasted;
especially if you have more to give

That's primarily why I make a conscious effort to
write words to uplift men

Or when someone needs a helping hand, I've always
got one to lend

Know that I'm being sincere when I say, I wish us
all well and we should strive for peaceful unity

I say it for all mankind, not just those in my
community.

Before My Daughters Were Born

Though I've never met her, I am really glad she
belongs to me
Don't want to control her; just console her when
her tears flow you see
I'd do my best to put a smile on her face
whenever she feels to frown
I'd be that father figure to lift her spirits
whenever she is feeling down
I'd respect and protect her because that's what
father's do
I'd show her how a man should treat her if for
her his love is true
I'd encourage her to always avoid idle gossip
because it really is a destructive force
I'd tell her to be careful of what she hears or
reads and to always consider the source
I'd do my absolute best to help her achieve her
desired success
I'd show her with my actions that her existence
further proves I am blessed
I'd be a friend indeed whenever she needs by
always giving her the facts
I'd show her that she is worthy of unconditional
love by simply giving her that
I'd help strengthen her weaknesses while
strengthening her strengths
I'd do that and more for sure because I know she
is truly heaven sent.

Better To Struggle???

It appears to me that when people receive or accomplish things too easy, they tend to take it for granted when a good deed is done for them. I really believe we must let certain people struggle to accomplish their goals. Thereby making it more gratifying when their true potential is realized. Perhaps then, they will become better people. After all, we should all strive to be better people...............Shouldn't we?

Call A Friend

Call a friend today and ask if everything is ok

Just the concern alone (if it is genuine) will
brighten their day

We all have the power to help someone if we
really, really care

All we need do is realize that in our struggles, we
too would want a friend there

In good times and in bad, especially when we are
happy, mad or glad

A friend is someone I sincerely wish we all had.

Calling Card For Greatness

When we allow negativity to exist in our daily life,
it slowly pushes positivity out
That's why I don't associate with certain people;
that's just not what I'm about
So if you're into destroying, then you should know
you've destroyed the possibility of us being friends
But if you're creating and building, you've enhanced
the chances of us being friends til the very end.

Positive creativity is the calling card for greatness.

Challenging Times

We all go through challenging times; Lord knows
I've been through mine

And so I'm here to tell you that if this is your
time, you're gonna be just fine

In you, I see a person who can accomplish
whatever you put your mind to; you're pictures
reflect it

You will prevail, you will not fail though others
seem to want and at times expect it

They represent people trying to solve a mystery
about history when they haven't got a clue

In doing so, they prove themselves to be fools
when they bet against you

Guess you could say, I see potential for success in
every pic I see

I can say that as a fact because your pics are
reminiscent of a reflection of me.

Change is Necessary

When change is necessary, then a change should be made

If the joy felt in the past was real, then the memories will never fade

However, we should realize that everything that gives us pleasure isn't always good for us

Which is why change is not always an option; sometimes it is a must

And when we the storm called change begins to seem like a lite rain

its because the sun will soon shine as we focus on what we've gained.

CHILD SUPPORT AND THE POWERS THAT BE

I am often amazed at how the powers that be decide how much a man should pay for child support. I find myself wondering exactly what criteria is used when deciding how much the child should receive.

Whatever the criteria is, I think it should be used when the father is deceased and the government decides the family is eligible for public assistance or welfare, as it is commonly known. Obviously it isn't. Why the double standard?

I also wonder why the effort to make sure their fathers support the children is not matched by some type of system or agency to make sure the money collected is in fact used for the children. After all, it is a waste of taxpayer's money to make the effort to track down deadbeat dads, then garnish their checks and not make sure the money is being spent on the children.

Aren't we all taught that we should always get a receipt when we spend our hard earned money? Why doesn't the same rules apply when paying child support?

I think anytime men are fortunate enough to father children, they should support the child. They should give moral, emotional and financial support. When they are unwilling to give support, it is a clear indication that they are not taking the blessing of fatherhood as seriously as they should. Whenever possible, they should always support the child they helped create.

When a man makes a conscious effort to avoid supporting their child financially, I think he should be punished. So too should any woman. When a woman decides to spend money that is designated for the child on something else other than the child, I think it is wrong. I really think it is stealing. I actually think she is stealing not from the father of the child. I think she is actually stealing from the child. Therefore she should be punished to the full extent of the law!!!

Church, A problem?

Some people say they don't go to church because they don't want to be near a bunch of hypocrites. So for them, church is a problem. I really don't think the problem is the church or the people in it. I believe our expectations of people who choose to attend church on a regular basis is the problem. I think we expect people to be different because they are doing something that deep down we all know we should be doing. Trying to get closer to God.

We must all understand that those people who choose to attend church are people first. Thus they are just like us. They make mistakes and bad decisions too. The difference is they are going to the house of the lord to ask for guidance and forgiveness.

Comfort Zones

The fact that many of us are unwilling to leave our comfort zone, often times contribute to our inability to set and ultimately accomplish goals. The fact is, the likelihood of us setting and possibly achieving those goals improve dramatically when we voluntarily abandon our old comfort zones to create a new one, which is conducive to the success we aspire to achieve.

Consistently Inconsistent

When a person is consistently inconsistent, it is probably because they aren't persistent in their attempts to become consistent, thereby adding clarity to as to why they are consistently inconsistent. With that being said, we need to be consistent in our attempts to acknowledge and accept their inconsistencies........That thought process will help us avoid disappointments.....Consistently, I might add.

Contenders & Champions

Contenders sometimes get knocked down;
champions ALWAYS get up

Contenders are sometimes weak; champions are
ALWAYS tough

Contenders sometime want to do certain things;
champions ALWAYS find a way to get things done

Contenders aren't sure if they can win;
champions ALWAYS believe the game isn't over
until they've won

Contenders get weary when uncertainty remain;
champions ALWAYS gain strength when success
is within range

Contenders sometimes do nothing but complain;
champions ALWAYS have the courage to make a
necessary change.

Like many of you reading this, I too am a
"CHAMPION"!!!

Continue Your Trial!

One day you treat me right, then later you treat me
rotten.
And because you apologize at night, you think all is
forgotten?
Though at times I can forgive, I hardly ever forget.
I can remember all that you did, what else would
one expect?
Fortunately, I have God in me and I wish he were
with you too.
Perhaps then my friend you wouldn't choose to do
the things you do.
But you are who you are; your ways will remain the
same.
To make things right and enhance my life, it is I
who must make a change.

So now I keep to myself because I like to be alone.
Because when I choose to trust others, their
dishonesty is usually shown.
For that reason, I will not rely on any person at all.
Instead, the heavenly father is who I now choose to
call.
I don't even need a phone, for there is no need to
dial.
He alone will judge me as he sits on the throne. So
without me, continue your trial!!!!!

Created Equal

I write words of wisdom that I hope will inspire.
The fact that I can, should be proof to every man
that the devil is a liar.
All we need to do is live good with each other daily.
So each day I pray to God because unlike man, he
has never failed me.
He knows all things and he hears all people.
My God doesn't have favorites; which is why he
created all men equal.

Decisions

Decisions have to be made whether they are tough
ones or not

When we focus on our options we need be thankful
for the choices we've got

So whenever a decision has to be made, we are
better served to simply embrace it

The consequences of tough decisions are inevitable,
so we might as well just face it

Once we accept that fact, we should make a
decision after thinking everything through

It's a state of mind that works well for me and I
know it'll work well for you too.

Disappointment Continues

When someone disappoints you more than they exceed your expectations, it is probably because you are not yet disappointed in yourself for believing they'd never disappoint you. Therefore, the disappointment inevitably continues.

DNA Of My Soul

How many people would actually fail if we all lend
a helping hand?
I am willing to blaze a new trail as I try to
encourage every man.
We should love, cherish and treat our women with
respect.
Be there always for our children, never let them feel
neglect.
The practice of helping others must begin at home.
If we all understood that, then perhaps when we are
by ourselves, we would never feel alone.

I usually try to shed a positive light on a negative
situation when I can.
Often times, I do it in ways most people can
understand.
I simply remember, that it could always be worse.
I always pray to God too, yes is he whom I confide
in first.
He is never too busy, nor does he ever put me on
hold.
He is the reason I am who I am, a simple man; he is
the DNA of my soul.

Do A "Good Deed"

Encourage someone else and you instantly improve
yourself

There is no better feeling than positively making
your existence felt

I can say that because in my heart I know it's really
true

So each day I pray that I may stay positive in all
that I do

And when I have a free moment, I post a thought
for others to read

Because if motivating others to succeed is good,
then I'll do a good deed

Do Unto Others

"Do unto others as you would have them do unto
you", is a phrase I've often heard

That's why when some so call friends do certain
things, it is as if they've never heard those words

That's the only way I could rationalize why some
people do the crap they do

Then have the nerve to expect unconditional love
and respect from you

The truth is, you get what you give; some people
call it karma and I tend to agree

So I do my best to respect others so others will
be inclined to respect me.

Does True Love Ever Die?

Yes!!!

People who say, "true love never dies" have never been disappointed or betrayed repeatedly by someone they felt they truly loved.

Exercising in Traffic???

That moment when someone tries to encourage you to continue taking care of your body after they have run a few Miles in traffic before smoking a cigarette or two while sipping on Hennessy at 8:13 in the morning.

My Response:

If you are not gonna practice what you preach, you should be the last to speak

If a silent truth is a strong sense of self, then your vocal hypocrisy makes you incredibly weak

Your desire to puff on a cancer stick when it's lit or Hennessy on the rocks has got to stop cause it just can't be good

So don't worry about what I or another brother is doing with our bodies until you have learned to respect yours the way you should!!!

Eyes Wide Shut

When some of us cant see negative things or people coming, it's because our eyes are wide shut

Then when we can't explain why things went wrong for us, we tend to chalk it up as bad luck

The truth of the matter is many of us see daylight even if the sun has set and we can see the stars at night

That's a clear indication that we are living in the past so the future will never be right or bright

Instead, we need only concentrate on the here and now while using the past as a source of motivation when things seem hopeless

We must never be ashamed of where we came from but we must use those memories as a tool to help us remain focused

So when negativity begins to make the sounds that will undoubtedly cause us to make an unplanned detour, We should turn a deaf ear

I really don't mind seeing negativity as long as its through a mirror and its positively a reflection of the rear.

Forever Changing

Our lives are forever changing; nothing ever stays
the same

Memories of the way things use to be are all that
seems to remain

That's the moment when we wish we knew then
what we think we know now

Which leads us to believe things could and would
be different someway, somehow

Things may have been better or worse; we'll never
truly know for sure

But the fact is, the pain associated with change is
something we must all endure

At times, we may feel alone and the process may
even seem strange

But trust me when I say, we are all destined to
experience the phenomenon I call change.

Giving "Props"

Giving props to the single moms who raise their
children alone when a man is not a man

Giving props to the single dads who teach their
boys to be men when others doubt he can

Giving props to the daughters who make her mom's
love stronger just by reminding her of her younger
self

Giving props to the sons whose presence inspires
his father to have paternal feelings of love and
loyalty he's never before felt

Giving props to the grandparents who are stern and
firm, yet always know their place

Giving props to the parents who introduce their
children to the miracle of God's grace.

God's Grace

God's grace put me to sleep last night when I was
tired and yawning.

God's grace also woke me up early this morning.

So now as I travel on these lonely roads, I never
travel alone

I feel I can bear any load because God's grace has
truly been shown

So when life treats me roughly and I don't think
I'll finish the race

Just believe you can trust me when I say, "I
depend on God's Grace".

Going To See A Denzel Movie

My partner "JOHN Q" texted me this morning and asked me if I saw "THE EQUALIZER" yet? I told him no. Then I decided to wake my son and daughter and take them with me. My son fell back asleep and I told him to hurry up because we are almost "OUT OF TIME". Then all of a sudden he started getting dressed and running through the house like he was a "MAN ON FIRE". He did a "RICOCHET" off the hall wall before he got to the bathroom. Lol. When that happened, my daughter just laughed as she said, I guess this isn't a "SAFE HOUSE" anymore. Lol. I then asked her if she was ready. Her reply was hilarious. She told me if I saw a "DEVIL IN A BLUE DRESS" in the van, it means she is ready. (SMH). At that point, I reminded them both that we needed to hurry up because I know it's gonna be crowded and we don't have an "INSIDE MAN" to get our tickets. They just laughed as they said, dad we know you are gonna see this movie with or with out us because we know when you make your mind up about something, you are " UNSTOPPABLE". I just looked at my son and said, if knowing my habits is a basketball movie, I guess about you I'd be forced to say, "HE GOT GAME". Any way, we left to go to the theater but we drove instead of "TAKING PELHAM 123". Traffic was crazy. If I could've, I definitely would've caught the fastest "FLIGHT". When we arrived, there were a lot of people. It was almost as if there was a

"SEIGE" or something. I gave serious thought about blasting my way through until I realized I didn't have my "2 GUNS". That's when I decided to listen to some "MO BETTER BLUES" on my IPad while I flip through the pages of "THE BOOK OF ELI". The only reason I am standing in this line to see this movie is because I think Denzel Washington should be considered to be an American treasure that is not in need of another "TRAINING DAY" as far as his acting is concerned. If making a great movie is a war, we should all listen as he tells "A SOLDIER'S STORY" because as an actor, he personifies the term, "COURAGE UNDER FIRE".

Gotta Keep Pushing

Gotta keep pushing, even when it seems like I'm
going up hill

My ancestors had it harder; which means, I've got
big shoes to fill

Though at times I may miss a step and occasionally
even stumble

Confidence in myself is like my faith in the "Most
High"; it too will never crumble

So if there are negative things said or done that
would make a lesser man feel hopeless

I ignore what I've heard or saw and on the task at
hand, I remain focused.

Happy People

Happy people are really easy to notice.
When I look in the mirror I see one, that's really
how I know this.
Happy people try to make others happy too.
I know this to be true about me, and I hope it is true
about you.
If we all strive for happiness, perhaps one day we
will achieve.
We must pray day and night and in our God above,
we must always believe.

An OG (Original Gangsta) like me

They say I need detention because my lines are sick
But I get your attention with the rhymes I spit
Now you know I write poems, but some of you all
don't know
So I think it's time I show'em how an OG flow
Tell you about yourself like nobody else, you'll
never be the same
I might sound sinister but I am a minister in this
spoken word game
Oh my bad, this ain't no game, step to me and
you'll never achieve fame
You'll just get knock down clown but by the best
poet around, what a shame
My mike is like a gun and I'll execute ya
My lyrics are hollow point son, best believe I'll
shoot ya
I never miss with the shit I spit
My brain is insane; I got a full clip
So back up son cause I'm about to spray
I'm not givin a damn son, I'll ruin ya day
I'll take your pride with well aimed lyrics
I force feed you with the truth bro; even if you don't
wanna hear it
How you gonna hold a mike in your hand when you
know you wanna run
How you gonna look at a grown ass man and be like
"what up son"
What the in the world is wrong with you, you seem
confused
How you gonna try to play me when I done did
things you aspire to do

Remember as far as a female is concerned, you never had none
I guess you're the male version of the virgin Mary
ain't never had none but calling another brother son
Get the hell outta here with that before you get smacked
You expect me to respect you when your lying rhymes are whack
What are you stupid or cupid but then a gain cupid was stupid
Flying around town shooting people in the ass with arrows proves it
Don't worry, I'm gonna let you live but only on life support
I got no more time to give, I'm tired of going to court
I hope you listened and learned the lesson real well
Cause despite what you think you poetic game is in the toilet yeah homey it smells
So now I bruised ya ego cause that's how we go you had no luck with me
You should've started by asking what really happens when you step incorrectly an OG like me
Son!!! Excuse me did i say son? My bad, you ain't no kin to me
You cant even have what I had, you don't deserve that it B
Every word out your mouth is n----r this n----r that
To you, history is a mystery, it's obvious black
You need to expand your vocabulary and delete the word n----r from it
Even I am not exempted; I too am sometimes tempted but I rise above it

So until you try to be the best you can be, you can't
even try to step to me
You should be saying to yourself and everybody
else that it's a blessing to know a legend like this
OG.

His Hands.........

I've put all negativity behind me; yeah, I plan to
only take positive steps

I will have success without hurting another in
the process, so I wont have regrets

I'm just gonna do me; cause when I do, best
believe things get done

All the while in my own unique style, I give praise
to God's only begotten son

For he has carried me when others dropped me
and then chose to disrespect me

But being the man that I am, I understand his
hands will hold and always protect me.

Amen.

HOW CAN WE?..........
PERHAPS WE CAN.

How can we make the world a better place?
How can we put a smile on every child's face?
Perhaps we can change the world by the way we
choose to live.
Perhaps we can brighten a child's smile with the
love and affection we give.

How do we stop the war overseas, which affects
you and me?
How do we dry a young man's eyes as he cries
because his child has died so violently?
Perhaps we can teach love and respect to all to
prevent the murder of a son.
Perhaps we can save the lives of people we never
heard of, if we try to live as one.

How can we say we want to be trusted, when we
always seem to lie?
How can we say we want to go to heaven, yet none
of us want to die?
Perhaps we can one day be trusted, if from now on
we spoke the truth.
Perhaps we can all get to heaven, if we do what we
are suppose to do.

How Will You Be Heard?

Those who speak loudly while doing absolutely nothing simply want to be heard. Those who are doing positive things in silence will always be heard.

I Do My Best

I do my best to always write and post what I think is
right

Thereby bringing the finish line to negativity in
view when it seems out of sight

So for all those who aren't sure exactly how things
are gonna go

Remember, life is what we make it; that's something
we should all know

Positive reading promotes positive thoughts which
ultimately yields positive results

That fact is also true for children and teens; it is not
limited to adults

So we should all be mindful of what we read, post
and share on social media sites

Since we never know who we may be influencing,
it's best to try and do what's right.

I Don't Have Much Money But I'm "RICH"

An uplifting message can provoke a positive
thought

It has a priceless effect when heard; it cannot be
bought

That means most of us are rich already and we don't
even know it

We can all show our true worth if when we spoke,
we chose to show it

Do your best to show everyone your portfolio by
what you choose to do and say

They may really be impressed if you impacted
someone's life in a positive way

I Give Praises............

I give praises to the man above; yes, praises to
the man above only
It's my choice to rejoice when I think about the
love he has always shown me
I think about the tough times he's carried me
through when I couldn't stand tall at all
Even when I was losing my balance while
swaying in life's high winds, he never let me fall
There were times when things really got difficult
and I was beginning to feel somewhat hopeless
As the world got colder, he would tap me on my
shoulder and remind me to stay focused
Even as familiar faces tend to look strange, I
know he truly cares for me;
While some friends and family start to change, I
know he'll always be there for me
Since we are all created equally, it means he'll be
there for you always too
Just be sure to always stay pure and let God's
goodness come through you.

I Like Consistency!!!

People who remain consistently inconsistent are more likely to have inconsistent relationships with people they may actually care about.

The fact is, consistency gives others a peek at our character, which ultimately helps them determine whether or not we can be trusted. Without trust, there really is no relationship.

With that being said, I'd really prefer for my inconsistent acquaintances to consistently stay away from me.

I'd much rather continue to build and strengthen my relationships with those who are consistently trying to do the same with me.

Can you tell I like consistency???

I Miss Her

I miss her more than words can ever say, so I keep
those sentiments to myself
Still, the thought of time spent with her prevents me
from thinking of anyone else
Angels deserve a man who will strive for perfection
and yet I was far less than that
And so I lost the opportunity to be more than
friends; what a sad unfortunate fact
I wonder if she knew how much she meant to me;
would my, love still make her smile?
Perhaps she didn't take me seriously when I said
"babe, I really like your style"
I guess I'll never get the answers to any of the many
questions; she'll never say
I can't help but ask myself, where we'd be you see if
I treated her the right way
But I must admit that I'm missing her dearly
because she isn't near me; just another form of hell
Now she is gone to be happy with another lover and
all I can do is wish her well.

I Stay Strapped

I write these words to make a difference in this
world
I write in a way that is understood by every man,
woman, boy and girl
To each, I teach peace with the words I write and
speak
If silence caused by deadly violence makes you
strong, then I intend to make you weak
Negative vibes lead to death and ultimately a wake
Positive vibes save lives; makes us all strong as if
we're lifting weights

With that strength we could lend a helping hand to
someone who is falling behind
If I were that person, I'd want your hand reaching to
grab mines
That's why I choose to treat people the way I wish
to be treated
Helping all mankind is a goal of mine; I won't be
defeated!
I know the devil is busy but I don't worry about that
My faith is my ammunition; and you know,
"I STAY STRAPPED"!!!

If Her Eyes…

If her eyes reflect the possibility that for us there is
still hope
Then perhaps I'll find strength in that, so I too may
cope
If her eyes reflect a confidence that is surpassed
only by self esteem
Then perhaps I should look into my own conscience
and cherish my Nubian Queen
If her eyes reflect a respect that is always demanded
and never denied
Then perhaps I'll find a way to comfort the soul
when her eyes start to cry
And when her eyes reflect a forgiving heart, which
is why I love her so much
Then perhaps I'll cherish all of her qualities, not just
her touch
If her eyes reflect the love and kindness embodies
her soul
Then it's her beauty from within that my eyes now
behold
If her eyes reflect what I interpret as loves burning
passion
Then I pray to my God above that this vision will be
everlasting

If Positive Is..........

If a positive place is where you're going, you best
believe I'm with it
If opportunity is a fast ball, out of the park is where
I intend to hit it
If a motivating word needs to be heard, in poetic
form is how I'm gonna spit it
If igniting the candle of love is a crime, you best
arrest me cause I'm the one that lit it
If a soul is out of control and feeling low, I say and
do whatever it takes to uplift it
If spirituality is a garment, I wear it proudly like no
other brother; I call it custom fitted

If The Truth Will Set Us Free

If the truth will set us free, it's no wonder many of
us feel as if we are in prison

Lies upon lies affect our ability to receive and
believe when someone shares wisdom

That's why I choose to ride and die with the man
who resides above the skies

The "Most High" encourages me to speak the truth
to the youth instead of telling lies

So while many of us choose to omit the truth when
it seems to suit us best

There are times some may not want it but I gotta
keep it 100; that means less stress

So for all those people who want to be treated as
equals, give now what you want in return

Because negative karma in the form of lies and
disrespect is a wildfire where you too will
eventually get burned.

It's A Must!!!

If a person makes you feel more special, it is
because you are special to them

So if you both fight to unite, it's not a matter of if
it'll happen but a matter of when

But if a person makes you feel as if you are always
a distraction

I find its a waste of time; trust me, pursuing them is
a wasted action

We'd all be better off if we found someone who
wants to be with us at all cost

I'd say that's the best way to prevent time and
sometimes friends from being lost

But instead, we continually pursue those who really
aren't interested in us

Change is not an option if we want different results
adults; IT'S A MUST!!!

Keep Things Simple

I like to keep things simple; that's the way I choose
to express myself

So simply, yet poetically I encourage others to
positively make their presence felt

With life comes the opportunity to enhance the lives
of others; let's face it

We can all make the choice to do good by following
our instincts which are forever basic

Instead, some of us have ill will towards others and
even wish they'd crash & burn

Then we have the nerve to be in search of someone
with a fire extinguisher when it becomes our turn

I really wish we all understood that our thoughts
and actions help determine our destiny

If we all did, perhaps when lightening strikes, I
wouldn't care who was standing next to me.

Let Me Love You.........

Let me be that special friend that will hold your
hand when you need someone to lead
Let me love you
Let me guide you when your sense of direction
requires someone else to lead
Let me love you
Let me advise you when you need a creative
suggestion to help you succeed
Let me love you
Let me be that person to give you constructive
criticism as you strive to succeed
Let me love you
Let me comfort you in that moment you need to be
comforted most
Let me love you
Let me be that person to encourage your faith in the
times you need it most
Let me love you
Let me be the one to pick you up when others are
hell bent on putting you down
Let me love you
Let me be the person you call when you can't get up
after you have fallen down
Let me love you
Let me be the person with the listening ears when
everyone else is deaf and your words need to be

heard

Let me love you

Let me be the person standing next to you when you
succeed and your celebration of triumph needs to be
heard

Let me love you

Let me love you

Let me love you

Life Is About Choices

Life is about choices; life is about making good
decisions

Life is about listening to our inner voices telling us
to get away from those who cloud our visions

Life is about learning from things that went wrong
when we were trying to do right

Life s about rising from the darkness of betrayal to
appreciate unconditional love and it's light

Life is a blessing and should be cherished by those
who are fortunate enough to live

Life shouldn't be measured by how many
materialistic things we receive but instead by how
much kindness we give.

LIFE IS ALSO ABOUT.........

Life is about learning each and everyday we live

Life is about giving in to the temptation to always give

Life is about spreading knowledge and encouraging others to do the same

Life is about realizing none of us are perfect and never feeling shame

Life is about building people up while never tearing anyone down

Life is about putting a smile on a face that seems to always have a frown

Life is about wishing the same for others as we'd wish for ourselves

Life is about not being negatively influenced by those who don't respect themselves.

LIFE IS LIKE AN ORCHESTRA

All failures I'm leaving, and to success I'm coming.
I'm not an acoustic guitar, nor am I strumming.
I be the man with the plan, it will be a surprise to
some.
As tears are shed as I wake the dead when I kick the
bass drum.
So you can play your piano or some type of horn.
Success is part of my DNA, which defines my
destiny from the day I was born.

Life Teaches Us

Often times life teaches us, even when we don't
want to learn

Today I'm in class, tomorrow could very well be
your turn

We should look at life's challenges and
disappointments as "school in session"

That way we could look at what it takes to
overcome them as Gods greatest blessings

So it really doesn't make sense to cry and stress
over things we cannot control

Because obstacles, challenges and disappointments
are nourishment for the soul

Those things all serve a purpose; like vitamins &
minerals, they all make us stronger

Now that I realize that, I stay blessed and I am
stressed no longer.

Live As One

A peaceful society is something I truly yearn for
It can only happen if about each other we learn
more
We should learn our differences because it will lead
to respect
Perhaps then when someone is not like us, it's their
uniqueness we would accept
Thereby getting rid of the fear that leads to hatred
by some
Making it possible for us all, to live as one

Lose To Gain More

There are times when we must lose who we
thought we liked or even loved to gain more

If consistency is absent by another but important
to us; a change is necessary, that's for sure

We've all heard "life is short" and many of us
would agree, it's getting shorter by the minute

That's why I feel we must respect our lives
enough to disassociate ourselves from those who
need not be in it

I also feel if we are committed to our search of
happiness, we'd make better decisions

We wouldn't allow lies or any other form of
deceit to ever again distort our vision.

Love Killers

Some of us don't realize we have the power to KILL love. Those are the people who are more likely to commit murder as far as romance is concerned.

Therefore, when the love we share with another is on life support, we usually don't see the symptoms. So we continue to do the very same things that will ultimately lead to the end of the relationship.

That's what usually happens when we choose not to cherish the phenomenon we call LOVE. We are more likely to KILL it!!!.....Since we are never arrested and subsequently convicted of murder, it is still very likely that we'll be sentenced to a life of misery if we lose what we consider to be the love of our life.

Unfortunately, many of us are or will become serial killers.

MY MANY BLESSINGS

God has carried me through life's roughest storms
even when I never left the house

Through the coldest of winters, though we had heat,
my God kept we warm; in him I shall never doubt

He has helped me to cross the most violent seas
though I never left land

Though my God is always silent he leads me with
ease by simply holding my hand

My God can't be seen and he isn't often heard

Though my God is a vengeful God, he is never
mean to those who live by his word

Whether I am happy, sad or even bored, there is a
supreme being that I will never question

I will keep trusting and believing in the Lord and
thanking him for my many blessings.

Men, Rise Up!!!

As men, we must rise above negative stereotypes by
first learning to love ourselves enough to take the
time to learn our history. Then and only then, will
we truly appreciate and ultimately honor the efforts
of our ancestors. We can begin by striving to be the
best sons, husbands, fathers, uncles and friends we
could possibly be. Thereby uplifting us as a race
and at the same time destroying those negative
stereotypes that affect us all.

Mind In The Gutter

I slid my fingers in; it felt so tight.
I wasn't sure if it still belong to me, I didn't feel
right.
I felt like I was sticking it in the wrong hole.
Yeah it felt warm, but it felt wrong to my soul.
I took my fingers out and slowly slid them back in.
Then I realized why the gloves didn't fit; they
belonged to my friend

Your mind was in the gutter wasn't it?

Mind Over Matter

Mind over matter is a positive way to approach any challenge that may seem impossible

I know that doing so doesn't eliminate the possibility of failure; it just makes it improbable

That's why I write and recite original scribes with the sole intent to provide encouragement

So if food for thought is what you need, you best believe I'm cooking up poetic nourishment

Yeah, I prepare what is read by the eyes but ultimately consumed by our soul

Just another indication that the "Most High" who resides above the skies is really in control.

Motorcyclist Without Helmets

Just watched a man get stopped by the police for not wearing his seatbelt while driving here in Texas. After giving the man a citation, the cop drove off and then stopped at the red light at the next corner. Another man on a motorcycle pulled up next to him. The police officer and the man on the motor cycle acknowledged each other with a wave........None of this is strange except for the fact that the motorcyclist wasn't wearing a helmet (it's legal but incredibly stupid to ride without a helmet here).......Hmmmmm, so I guess it's perfectly legal to have an accident while riding a motorcycle and having your brains scattered all over the road for unsuspecting bystanders (some of which may be children) to see, as long as you didn't get thrown from your vehicle because you weren't wearing a seat belt. That my friends would be illegal..........
SMDH

My Brother's Keeper

We could all be kinder to others, so that we can all have good day

I don't pretend to have all the answers; there are simply to many ways

Perhaps a motivating word or a simple pat on the back

Can ultimately provide the confidence a person now lacks

If that person succeeds it means for him the cost of success just became cheaper

Then and only then can I truthfully say, "I am my brother's keeper."

SHE MAY NEVER KNOW IT

There is a lady I truly love and she doesn't even
know it
I pray to my God above that one-day I'll be able to
show it
Although I see her everyday, seeing her is not
enough
A photograph of the time I made her laugh is good
but I yearn for her touch
I'd love to look into her eyes when I bring her
beautiful flowers
I'd like to give her a surprise when she steps out of
the shower
A soft kiss on the lips would be appropriate before I
told her about the cruise
We'd visit Jamaica, Grenada, Trinidad, Guyana, and
Barbados too
I'd do everything I could to make her happy
because she deserves it
And whenever she said she wanted breakfast in bed,
I'd be there to serve it
I'd do everything I could to let her know that I
would take her for granted no longer
I'd do all that I can to make her understand that
together we'd both be stronger

I really don't know if I'll ever get the chance to
prove my love again
Because we both have life, I guess it's really not the
end
I'll just have to continue to hope and pray
That she'll see me for who I am today
I really love the lady and I want the chance to show
it
All of this is just pipe dream it seems, for she may
never know it

My Personal Mission

When a person chooses not to accept changes, it is
sometimes best to leave them behind

We must never allow circumstances or another
person's issues determine how bright our star will
shine

Instead, we must continue on the path to success
hoping they will soon follow

Though in some ways, we wish it were today but
for some it may be tomorrow

Even though without knowing it, we can all
encourage others by our actions

Perhaps we can add to a person's self esteem by
performing a necessary subtraction

Yes, we can eliminate a person's self doubt by
helping them to believe in themselves

If we can reach them, then we can teach them to be
dependent on themselves and no one else

Though I am nowhere near being perfect, that is my
personal mission

That's why I write what I write, hoping a few will
choose to listen.

My Turn

Today, I miss some of the positive people in my life
who have now passed on

But I know I'll be ok because the good memories
live on

Yes, I can remember the love and the times we
shared

I remember how they gave me a hug or a call at the
right time simply because they cared

They truly meant a lot to me because they taught so
that I could learn

They made a difference in peoples lives, now it's
my turn.

No Chance Of Lasting

I'm not suppose to love her but I really think I do
Those are the two words I said to my wife when I
married her too
Although I'm still a married and I still love my wife
One night of weakness is now threatening my way
of life
I thought I was being discreet when I decided to
cheat
I'm like everyone else I couldn't help myself, I
guess I'd say I was weak
It's just that the lady was fine with a pair of thick
hips
On sight I had to make her mine, I had to kiss those
lips
While thinking about all the things that with her I
wanted to do
I had no idea that she was inspecting and checking
me out too
I watched as she smiled ever so slightly in my
direction
I thought about politely approaching what I thought
was perfection
One thing led to another and we did what
consenting adults do
I did so because I thought our feelings for each
other was true
Damn, I was wrong, this lady doesn't care
She is nothing like my wife; she won't always be
there

But this lesson was learned far too late; my wife has
now left with our kids
She has no idea how sorry I am that I chose to do
what I did
I lost everything I truly loved for a single night of
passion
And to think I did all of this for a relationship that
had no chance of lasting

No Pork? Mind your <u>OWN</u> business

Although some people were raised eating pork, many of them have made a conscious decision to stop eating it. Many have decided to stop for various reasons. Some people no longer eat pork because they have changed their faith and the new faith they have chosen prohibits the consumption of pork of any kind. Others have stopped eating it simply because they now think pork is not good for us.

Although I am still among the many people who love to eat bacon with my eggs in the morning or a nice ham and cheese sandwich with mustard for lunch, I must acknowledge the fact that pork is not a food that promotes good health. Still I choose to eat it. The operative words are "I choose to".

Because I choose to eat it, I really don't think I should have to listen to people bragging and boasting that they no longer eat pork. I really think they should keep their opinions to themselves. I say that because once I see them drinking an alcoholic beverage or puffing on a cigarette, their credibility on what is good or not good for anyone's body is a zero as far as I'm concerned.

Hypocrites always get that rating.

No Regrets

Live life to the fullest and do so with no regrets

Never look down on anyone; Everyone deserves
respect

Always set goals and always do your very best to
achieve them

If anyone tells you you're worthless, you must never
believe them

Always respect yourself so that others will follow
suit

Never do to another what you don't want done to
you.

No Time For Games

I've got no time for games; the clock is steady
ticking

Poverty is the ultimate bully; it's his ass I'm
steady kicking

He straight sucker punched me a few years back

He thought he landed a knockout blow but it was
more like a slap

So I remained on my feet and kept my guard up

Now work is like the sun; I can't seem to get
enough

So I'm up early this Saturday morning about to
start my shift

Thinking about a few things and being thankful
for the ultimate gift---LIFE.

NUMBERS: Odd and Even

1. Whenever we add two odd numbers together, the answer will always be an even number.
2. Whenever we add two even numbers together, the answer will always be an even number.
3. Whenever we add an even number and an odd number, the answer will always be an odd number.

One Life To Live

I'm living my life as if I've got one life to live

You see I understand what is, that's why I choose
to give

Whether is money, knowledge or just a helping
hand

I'll do whatever I can to help my fellow man

Can you imagine if everyone felt this way too?

You know, you always helped me and I always
helped you

I really believe we can all succeed if we all
understand what is

I wish we would all learn to give, because we all
have just one life to live.

Our First gift

Poetically gifted, yet spiritually motivated

Since I write from the heart, my thoughts will never
be duplicated

I don't like negative things that I believe disrespect
women

So if positive vibes is poison, then believe I spit
venom

We should treat all women with respect and always
show her love

If you know anything about the Bible, then you
know that a woman was the first gift to us from the
man above.

Perfectly Normal

When someone says that something is perfectly normal, I wonder if they realize a statement like that contradicts it self. Perfection is so rare that it really can't be considered normal.

Perhaps Today......

So many thoughts go through my mind in the dawn,
I can't wait for sunrise

Perhaps today is gonna be different; perhaps there'll
be a pleasant surprise

Perhaps today will be the first day where the world
is void of hate and envy

Perhaps we can finally find friendship with one we
now consider to be an enemy

Perhaps today is the day we can implement the
master plan to achieve peace on earth

Perhaps we'll finally understand that all the money
in the world doesn't equal what one life is worth

Perhaps today the scientist will find a cure for
Diabetes, Hypertension & Cancer

Perhaps we'll all become non-violent after realizing
that violence simply isn't the answer

Perhaps today is the day where we no longer tell
each other half truths & lies

These things and more are what cross my mind as I
wait for the sun to rise.

Picking On Us
For Not Wearing Seat Belts

It's a shame police officers stop us and subsequently give us tickets for not wearing seat belts. Perhaps it's because they simply don't have the manpower to stop every bus or train that transport people on a daily basis. After all, there aren't any seat belts on many buses and trains, particularly city buses. I guess they figure it's easier to pick on the small guy. I just don't like it when they insult our intelligence by telling us, "it's for our own safety". While that is true, I really think we'd be even safer if they gave the companies that provide their transport services to thousands of people tickets at the same rate for their failure to provide seat belts.....Then and only then would I feel that the powers that be truly cared about our safety. Until then, I feel like their picking on us.

Pipe Down Clown!!!

If many of us spoke less and chose to listen just a
little bit more

Heartaches that could be avoided would be avoided
for sure

But instead, many of us choose to speak about
things when we really don't have a clue

I'm sure those people not only interrupt me but they
interrupt you too

Those are the type of people who feel they need to
be both seen and always heard

Despite the fact that their opinions about a
particular subject usually seem absurd

To them I say, "Pipe down clown"!!!

Poetry & Love
(Something in common)

Poetry is like love. It can always be found but
when it is, those fortunate enough to experience
it rarely appreciate and cherish it.

Positive Blood

Positive blood flows through my veins after being
pumped by a kind forgiving heart

Though it might sound strange, nothing has
changed; I've been this way form the start

People always say, "it is what it is" but I can
honestly say, "I am who I am"

Though some question my motives, I remain a
positively encouraging man

Without effort, I'm able to appreciate the good in
people when others can only see the bad

I possess a sense of optimism that some frown on
but secretly wish they had.

Positive Energy

Positive energy fuels all that is right in this world

This is a fact that applies to men, women, boys and
girls

Therefore, we should all do our best to make sure
nobody's tank is on empty

By sharing positive vibes; because we are blessed
with life, there should be plenty

So when we communicate with others, we can
encourage another if only we make the choice

Just think about how uplifted we all feel when we
hear a positively uplifting voice.

Lift your spirits by lifting another.

Positive Poetic Expressions

Positive poetic expressions is just one quality that
make me unique

Blessed with the gift to uplift each with words I
choose to write or speak

So if your read or hear me, know that my words are
inspired by the "Most High"

Just spread your spiritual wings and you too can and
will ultimately fly

Just be sure to embrace the wind of preparation &
effort before your flight begins

Understand that as long as you give your best, the
beginning of success truly lies deep within.

Positive Steps

When we are fortunate enough to have someone
worship the ground we walk on, we should always
strive to take positive steps.

Positive Steps (2)

When this world seems to have us off balance,
our love for our children always seem to balance
life's scales

While we do our very best to help them go where
they want to go in life, l realize they are the wind
beneath my sails

They provide a genuine joy deep within that
simply can't be duplicated by any acquaintance
or friend

Sometimes I reminisce about their childhood; I
must admit, I do it quite often

I remember going Back and forth to Barbados
and giving them a kiss on the cheek as they slept
before I left

Since I know they worship the ground I walk on,
I do my absolute best to always take positive
steps

They are the perfect compliment to what's really
right with whatever I do or have already done

I can't thank God enough for blessing me with my
beautiful daughters and my handsome son.

Parents know the type of love I write about..........

Positive Thoughts

Lyrics that lifts spirits embodies the song that I sing

Positive vibes for all mankind is what I choose to
bring

You see life is about choices and although I am just
one man

To each I preach and teach to repeat after me when I
say, "I love who I am"

I'd say, positive thoughts are in my DNA

It helps me to overcome obstacles on any given day
when things aren't going my way

And when negative issues would have other people
feeling no longer straight but instead a little bent

I put my fingers on the keyboard and pray to the
lord to help me write at night to give me & others
strength.

Positively Energetic

Unfortunately negative vibes consume many of our
lives

Thank God I am the exception to the rule; I take
positive strides

I encourage others to do the same although I know
it is not the norm

So though negativity seems to surround me, I
simply refuse to conform

Though life can at times be cloudy, I maintain an
inner peace by always looking for that silver lining

So if I seem positively energetic, don't be alarmed;
it's just the "Most High" in me that is shining

Potential To Be Great

We all have the potential to be great, each in our
own way

It becomes more possible to realize that potential if
we pray each day

We can start by asking the man upstairs to help us
achieve unity

Thereby making this a better place to live for both
you and me

Let's make lies, jealousy, envy, prejudice, gossip &
rumors a thing of the past

So when we achieve the unity I dream about, it will
surely last.

Pretending To Be In Your Corner

Some people pretend to be in your corner when
they're not even in the room
They claim they'll brighten your day but are no
where to be found when it's filled with gloom
These are the facts of life as it pertains to certain
people
You'll never be friends til the end; they never looked
at you as being equal
So be very aware of the company you keep; for they
may not have your best interest in mind
Considering how accessible the "Most High" is, he
really isn't hard to find
Just bow your head and begin to give thanks for all
you have and you too shall be heard
Occasionally you can ask for things you want but
never let your desires dominate your words
Also remember that prayer without effort is a
conversation no one needs
After all, prayer is the foundation of success when
followed by the building blocks called effort, then
and only then do we truly succeed.

Private Thoughts

Private thoughts are and will always be at the root
of any great action
If showered with effort & persistence, the wheels
leading to success will gain greater traction.

Procrastination

So much to do and so little time left to do it

Only God and God alone can help us get through it

That's why procrastination is an enemy of mine

For when it is our friend, we seem to waste so much time

So we should keep it far away or shall I say, "at a distance"

We can achieve our goals if we befriend a thing called persistence

We must stay focused and choose our friends wisely

Remember

When you see a person in need and choose to pass
them by
How can you expect that in your time of need,
someone will hear your cry?
Life is about giving and making contributions.
If you don't, then others wont, its called paying
retribution.
So make a deposit, do a good deed.
Search your heart, make a start and help someone in
need.

Remember

Blessed is the man that chooses to help others.
Blessed are the children who love and respect their
mothers.
Blessed are the friends who soon become lovers.
Blessed are all the above who are always there for
one another.

Remember

Love for something or someone is normal for most
people.
That's why we should all have respect for each other
and treat everyone like equals.
Our differences should bring us closer but instead
divides some.
Perhaps if we all understood this, God's work can
truly be done.

Respect And Cherish Every Woman

All men should realize that we need to love, respect
and cherish every woman we are fortunate enough
to meet
For its a fact that if we did that, the word "BITCH"
would never be used when referring to them when
we speak
The truth of the matter is that a woman is not
inferior or superior but they make us whole in more
ways than I can mention
I guess one could say that when my mom was
showing me why a woman should be considered
equal, I payed close attention
She taught me that a woman can be supported by
and or supportive of her man and she can do it with
grace
She made this man understand that a woman doesn't
have to lag behind in the race we call life; she can
always keep pace
So for all the women who are an important part of
anyone's success be it man or woman, I'll simply
say, "NUFF RESPECT"
Perhaps if more of us thought the same, the reality
that women are in fact equal to men wouldn't be so
hard for many to accept.

Sad Idiots Farting

Idiots out number us, that is a sad fact

We should help them because they are lost,
perhaps they need a map

They don't know where they are and don't know
where they are going

Perhaps that's why they continue to talk as they
walk, without realizing their ignorance is
showing

Still, I pray for them because that is in my heart

I just hope they don't lose what's left of their
senses when they feel the need to fart.

SHE MAY NEVER KNOW IT

There is a lady I truly love and she doesn't even
know it
I pray to my God above that one-day I'll be able
to show it
Although I see her everyday, seeing her is not
enough
A photograph of the time I made her laugh is
good but I yearn for her touch
I'd love to look into her eyes when I bring her
beautiful flowers
I'd like to give her a surprise when she steps out
of the shower
A soft kiss on the lips would be appropriate
before I told her about the cruise
We'd visit Jamaica, Grenada, Trinidad, Guyana,
and Barbados too
I'd do everything I could to make her happy
because she deserves it
And whenever she said she wanted breakfast in
bed, I'd be there to serve it
I'd do everything I could to let her know that I
would take her for granted no longer
I'd do all that I can to make her understand that
together we'd both be stronger
I really don't know if I'll ever get the chance to
prove my love again
Because we both have life, I guess it's not the end
I'll just have to continue to hope and pray
That she'll see me for who I am today
I really love the lady and I want the chance to
show it
All of this is just pipe dream it seems, for she may
never know it

Shout to all The Women And Men

Shout out to all the women who post pictures that
show they are ladies

Shout out to the men standing up like men and
taking care of their babies

Shout out to all those who post positive messages
for others to read

Shout out to all those people who publicly yet
secretly do good deeds

Shout out to all the haters and non-believers; they
don't faze me

Shout out to all the fellas who are on their grind
thereby proving all men aren't lazy

Shout out to all the people who care enough to help
others succeed

Shout out to the men and women who aren't
followers because they realize they were born to
lead.

Simply Not Deserving

Some people say and do things that are for their
own personal gain

Which is why some say and do things that cause
others pain

We must beware of those who are guilty of the
above and do so with no remorse

They are not and will never be the type of friends
that will truly stay the course

Instead, they will say things to benefit them because
they are only self serving

It's a waste of time trying to befriend that kind
because they are simply not deserving.

Snakes In The Grass

Be kind to a stranger and a stranger may be kind to you

Always respect the blessings of friendship in all you choose to do

True friendship is rare, so we should cherish it when we've found it

And remember, positivity is a good thing, so choose to stay around it

Also keep in mind that the way a person treats you is based on how they perceive you

Be wary of snakes in the grass; they are put there by the devil and their sole intent is to deceive you.

Some Of Us

Some of us know exactly where we want to be
whether we are awake or asleep it seems

That's why I believe aspirations are almost always
preceded by dreams

Others simply grow into what they will eventually
become

Then there are those who take longer until they are
encouraged by some

The fact is, we all aspire to be something we are not

That's why we must all work hard to achieve goals
by using all that we acquire and all we've got

It's a fact that every goal is definitely achievable

The fact that so many goals are achieved everyday
makes this belief more believable.

Some People!!! I Tell Ya.........

Some people keep their mouths shut when it counts
then claim to be outspoken

Some people!!! I tell ya........

Some people say what's on their mind; then when
confronted, they claim they were just joking

Some people!!! I tell ya........

Some people claim they can fix anything and
anyone although they are the ones who are clearly
broken

Some people!!! I tell ya........

Some people claim they have new ideas; in reality,
their ideas are as obsolete as the NYC subway token

Some people!!! I tell ya........

Some people claim to be ok after a tragedy and
won't admit their having trouble coping

Some people!!! I tell ya........

Some people claim they pray things get better but
never bend their knees; they're actually just hoping.

Some people!!!

Something I Want To Mention

There is something that I want to mention

The time is right; now that I've got your attention

It's time for us to forget our differences and try to respect all

Otherwise, soon there'll be no trace of the human race; we'll all fall

The question is; are we gonna listen and learn and learn to listen?

Or are we gonna destroy each other despite the peace for which I'm wishing because unconditional love is missing?

Sometimes I.......

Sometimes I sit in the dark because it helps me to
see the light

Sometimes I watch others do wrong so that I can do
right

Sometimes I think about the moments I knew where
I was, yet still felt lost

Sometimes I think about the value of success and
I'm prepared to pay the cost

Sometimes I watch people who are sad so that I can
appreciate the times when I am not

Sometimes I reflect on times that I had nothing
because it helps me appreciate all I've got.

Spirit Lifters

If we all did our best to lift the spirits of someone
else

We'd not only be helping them, we'd be helping
ourselves

We should all say to another what we'd want to hear
if the situation were reversed

Blessings would come our way and it would happen
because it'd be well deserved

So let's treat people the way we truly want to be
treated because "KARMA" is real

And when we show kindness and compassion, it
enables a wounded soul to be healed.

Stand Tall

A man, who prepares himself to rise to the occasion when opportunity knocks, is a man who will always stand tall……….Even when he sits.

Stand Tall (2)

When we try to build ourselves up by tearing other people down, we actually succeed at showing everyone exactly how SMALL we really are.

Instead, we should all have confidence that we can uplift ourselves without criticizing and ridiculing others in the process.

If we did that, there is no doubt in my mind that there would be less SMALL people trying to stand tall at the expense of others.

Stay Out Of My Lane

I'm steady doing what I gotta do because certain
things gotta get done

Life is truly the best race on earth; so for what is
worth, I fully intend to run

And so I'm up early this morning ready to put in
some more work

Guess you could say I'm in training though at times
lack of sleep hurts

But I've often heard the phrase, "no pain, no gain"

I fully intend to be competitive in this race; if you
don't feel the same, stay out of my lane.

Staying Positive

Staying positive always is a personal goal of mine

So when mental toughness is required, I know I can
tow the line

In other words, I believe in my abilities regardless
of what others may sometime think

That's why my ship will always sail through life's
roughest storms while others tend to sink

I stay anchored in my faith; therefore, I'll never drift
from my positive ways

So in my darkest moments, the "The Most" is my
guiding light; to him, I give praise.

Straws, Why Do We Ask For Them?

When many of us go to a restaurant, most of us ask for a straw when we order a cold beverage with our meal. We do so because many of us don't want to put our mouths on the cup or glass it is served in. We'd much prefer to sip from a straw.

I wonder why we even bother to consume the beverage if we don't feel the glass or cup it is served in isn't clean enough to put our mouths on. The straw certainly doesn't help.

Since I believe the above is true, I am also left to wonder why is it that we seem to not mind sipping on a cup of tea, coffee or hot chocolate without ever having the same concerns.

Success Is My Destiny

Life provides challenges simply to build character
for both you and I

Overcoming those challenges lets us know we can
succeed if only we try

That's why we should always put our best foot
forward and the other right behind

For if "no effort" combined with "lack of
confidence" is dull, I have no choice but to shine

So regardless of the challenge, I'll keep that polish
called persistence in my pocket

Yes, it will always be next to me because success is
my destiny; nothing is gonna stop it!!!!

Sunday Morning Convo With Myself

People can say whatever they wanna say, for them too, I'll continue to pray

That's how I end my nights before I turn out the lights and it's also how I start my day

So while their spending time clocking me and knocking me

I'll continue to ride and die with the "Most High"; they ain't stopping me

So let them keep flapping their gums to some and I'll keep doing my thing

It's their negative words I'll ignore as I start to soar and explore when I spread my wings.

Superstitions

When someone says they believe in superstitions, I wonder if they believe in the Bible. The Bible says absolutely nothing about superstitions. As a matter of fact, the bible doesn't mention anything about good or bad luck.

I mean I can't find anything about a black cat, mirror breaking, umbrella openings in the house, walking under ladders or anything related to superstitions. So I guess it is not only unlikely but also impossible for someone to have faith in the Bible and still be superstitious. One thing contradicts the other.

Take A Shot At Success

I don't know how this day will end but I'm glad it began

Come any storm that may, it's that storm I'll withstand

As a matter of fact, I'll thrive while a lesser man would struggle to survive

Since every shot I take is contested, guess you could say I'm "battle tested" since I arrived

Still I can't help but think back about the days when success was for me only a wish

Since I like to score, now I want more; I just love to hear the net go Swisssshhhhhh.

Believe in yourself always!!! Take a shot at success.

TEMPERATURES DROP

I am often amazed at how negative some people can
be
I really think they do that because when they are
looking for potential, they avoid their reflection you
see
They see failure in themselves in some shape or
form
So in this cold world we live in. They use
discouragement to keep themselves warm
Personally, I hope those people freeze
I do my best to make their temperature drop by
doing my best to succeed.

THANK YOU JESUS

When we say, "thank you Jesus", is it because we
realize that we have been blessed?
Or do we say it because he has just pleased us and
we are preparing for yet another request?

Do we continually ask for things when we should
be giving thanks for all he has given us?
Are we sincere when it's his praise we sing or do
we sing because we feel we must?

Do we acknowledge the fact that God gave his only
begotten son so that we may live?
Perhaps the next time we say, "thank you Jesus" it
is because of the opportunity he gave us to give

Do we understand that today wasn't promised and
we are so very blessed to have it?
Do we really understand the meaning of thank you
Jesus or do we say it out of habit?

If we were aware that life is a movie and that
heaven is a sequel perhaps we'd be thankful then?
Maybe then we'd accept the fact that we are all
created equal and we are all God's children?

The 25th Of December

Let's not forget that on this date every year we
celebrate the birth of Jesus Christ

A man who despite the imperfections of man chose
for us to give his life

Yes, he died on the cross so that you and I may live

And so a poetic scribe to praise his name is what I
choose to give

We can begin to honor him all year, every year by
simply caring for each other

If we try, we can all find creative ways to motivate
and encourage another

Let's all be Christ like when we are approached by a
person in need

We need not ask, "what would Christ do?"; we
know he would've done a good deed

I am sure the world would be a much better place
for us all if only we could remember

To appreciate the life and the sacrifice of Jesus
Christ; and I don't mean only on the 25th of
December.

The Best Friend We've Got

Life teaches us lessons whether we want to learn or
not

Interactions with others reveal how many friends
we've got

The people we thought we could count on are never
there for us

They are usually there for themselves and others; so
for many, change is a must

We need not be bitter, instead we should accept
them for exactly who they are

The word unappreciative comes to mind based on
what they've shown us thus far

As sure as a tiger doesn't change his stripes and a
leopard doesn't change his spots

The creator of the universe should come first
because he's the best friend we've got.

The Devil Is Never Winning

I keep a positive state of mind so the Devil is never winning

Staying with God is never hard because he's the end and the beginning

So if you don't have something positive to say, by me you won't be heard

So bringing that nonsense to me is a waste of breath; Yeah, a waste of words

So be sure to hold your corner and I'll be sure to hold mine

Simply put so that it's understood; if it's negative, I don't have time

So if your heading my way, turn around and find a short plank and take a long walk

I don't mean to upend or offend anyone but in this scribe of mine, I gotta give you REAL TALK!!!!!

The Gift Of Encouragement

Life is about learning and learning improves quality
of life

Though none of us will ever be perfect, life is better
when we try to get it right

That's why it's so very important for us to help
others as much as we can

And so I choose to write about encouraging our
fellow man

For if we encourage him to always encourage
another

I guarantee there'll be significantly less jealousy and
hate towards any other

I will try to have a positive impact on how we all
will ultimately live

And so I hope the gift of encouragement is what we
all try to give.

The Key To Happiness

In order for us to unlock our own happiness, we
must all realize that we hold the key
That's why I can't deny that I can now confide that
the joy I search for is within me
No longer will I wait for others to accept and
appreciate me for I am
I consider it their lost if they can't understand that I
am a damn good man
A man who encourages others to forgive and at
times even to forget
To live their lives in a way so that towards the end
of the day, it is not filled with regret
Writing words that are enlightening when they are
heard truly makes me happy
I am so glad I found the key within me; now I can
show it for the world to see.

The Past Is The Past

The past is the past and perhaps that's where it
belongs

We've gone through the pain and now we stand
strong

And so now we shed no more tears; yes, our eyes
are dry now

So if life is a field of dreams, it's new grounds we
look to plow

Fresh seeds of love & affection planted can now
grow into flowers that last forever

But only if the memories and ties to the past have
some how been severed

Because if we dwell on the negative of the past, we
will never be strong

That's why I said, "the past is the past and perhaps
that's where it belongs".

THEY CLOCK ME AS THEY WATCH ME

Some people clock me as they watch me
And get mad because they just can't stop me
They can't influence what I'm doing or even where
I'm going
It's only themselves they are fooling as I keep the
words flowing

You see my destiny is fueled by strength and
perseverance but most of all desire
It will be guided by the knowledge and wisdom I
will surely acquire
No matter how much some may try, I won't be
denied
I'm in it to win it; my potential has no limit, just
like the sky

So when some people talk about me it is usually the
ones that tend to doubt me
Then when I succeed they act as if they can't live
without me
I don't even get mad when they try to knock me
because they're not me
As a matter of fact I feel sad for those that clock me
and watch me

Things Are Not Always The Way They Seem

Friendships are sometimes tested by decisions we
all make

Chance sometimes yield positive rewards unless it's
a foolish one we take

Pie is never satisfying when we truly have a taste
for cake

When a person trips, it may be funny until we
realize they aren't even awake

It can hurt if you dive into what looks like the ocean
but is really a shallow lake

Some people claim to hate reptiles but walk around
with their pet snake

Some of us think we are cooked well done with
common sense but many of us are only half baked

Those same people think they're always standing on
solid ground until the earth starts to quake.

Those Who Bet Against Me

For all those who bet against me; guess what, you
lose

Since life is about options, be careful in all that you
choose

The odds will always be in my favor because I
worship the Holy Saviour

So no matter what you say or do, my faith in him
shall never waiver

Time Doesn't Leave But It Goes

Where does the time go?

Does anyone really know?

Time waits on no man, yet man continues to waste time.

Because I truly understand, I wont waste mine.

I will simply do all I can with the time I am given.

Thereby giving thanks to the man above for keeping me among the living.

Waste Not, Want Not

Some say, "waste not, want not" so I do my best
not to ever be wasteful

And through all of life's challenges, I'll always
remain faithful

That enables me to appreciate what I've earned
while working to achieve more

Those qualities combined with positive thoughts
and prayers keep me grounded for sure

The best part is that I know many of you reading
this feel exactly the same way

Because we do, I know that enhances our
chances of having a productive day.

We Must Reformat Our Inner Hard Drive

Sometimes we endure a lot just to make things the
way they were before

If it wasn't good back then, why do we constantly
crave for more

There comes a time when we have to say good bye
to the past

And be sure to relive it only as long as the
memories last

We shouldn't try to recreate the past if it has led to
us not being happy now

Instead, we should realize change is now necessary;
some way, some how

We could or perhaps even should delete those
desires to be with certain adults

Yeah, we must reformat our inner hard drive if we
truly want better results.

We Shouldn't Be……..

We shouldn't be extremely negative and expect positive results

We shouldn't act like children and expect to be treated like adults

We shouldn't be against exercising and expect to be in great shape

We shouldn't be thoughtless and expect respect for decisions we make

We shouldn't be anti-social all the time and expect to have friends

We shouldn't expect to owe everybody and then question why friends don't lend

We shouldn't expect to be forgiven if we are still doing the same crap

These are just a few of my opinions that should be considered facts.

What Is Your Ride Sitting On?

I wish the average person who makes the decision
to remove the original rims from their car and
replace them with off the market rims were aware
that it could lead to dangerous and sometimes fatal
accidents.

In addition, the off the market rims expedite the
wear and tear process on their car. Things such as
brake pads, shocks, springs, struts axels and more
are directly affected by the off the market rims.

You see, the rims that came with the car when it
was delivered to the dealer from the manufacturer
have been tested and approved specifically for that
vehicle by the automotive engineers who designed
the car. Thereby making them much safer than most
and possibly all off the market rims that are usually
not tested by the engineer that designed your car.

When I consider the fact that many of us actually
take pride in wearing original name brand clothes
such as jeans, blouses, shoes, shirts and sneakers, I
am somewhat confused when I realize that we don't
take the same pride at keeping the original rims on
our vehicles although we all know that at some
point we will be going 55-75 miles an hour the first
chance we get.

What will be your answer when someone asks you that suddenly famous question: "what is your ride sitting on?" Hopefully you'll be able to truthfully say "originals".

What Do You See?

In most cases, the greatest person any of us will ever have the privilege to meet and subsequently interact with on a daily basis, stares us in the mirror when we look at a it. Unfortunately, many of us simply don't see greatness in ourselves. Thus we look for greatness in others. That is proof positive that many of us are in serious need of an EYE EXAM.

Put on your self-confident glasses or contact lens and take a look in the mirror......After seeing greatness in myself, I can honestly say, I see greatness in you too. The question is, what do you see?

When A Man Helps Another

When a man helps another, he also helps himself

A kind deed is what leads to good feelings being felt

It also increases our self worth when we choose to
lend a helping hand

Oh what a feeling, when we can help a fallen man
stand

For we know not what tomorrow brings; it may be
our turn next

That's why it's never good to judge anyone; instead,
treat all with respect

After all, what goes around, comes around; that's
what I have always heard

If we do for someone else, our existence is felt:
that's why I write inspiring words.

When My Mother Died

I cried inside when my mother died
I thought she'd always be with me but to myself I
lied
I now know I was wrong for my mother has passed
on
Now there are just plenty of wishes as I reminisce
about times that are forever gone

I can remember the sincerity in her face
As she told me I was her saving grace
She told me to always search for happiness and to
be sure to protect it
She taught me the definition of unconditional love
and to always respect it

I'd give anything to have her wake me singing rise
& shine again
Or to have her warn me about people I thought were
my friends
As she demonstrated a strong belief in faith and she
was always courageous
Since I now try to emulate some of her ways, I'd
say it was contagious

Although I thank god for the memories, I wish I
could create more
Am I needy or just greedy? I am not really sure
Am I needy because I feel lost without mom's
guiding hand?

Or am I greedy because I want her to continue
teaching me to be a good man?

I always considered a conversation with mom to be
somewhat of lesson
That is why I feel that when I was born to my
mother that it was my first blessing
These are just a few reasons why
I cried inside when my mother died

When Respect Has To Be Demanded

When respect has to be demanded, the reality of a
fake friendship becomes real

A relationship lost could be the cost when one feels
the need to express how one feels

When we have to demand respect, it's usually
because an individual has none for us

Though it use to seem that life without them would
be a negative, now we see it as a plus

And so we move on with our lives thereby leaving
them in the rear view mirror

Upon realizing and accepting that, life becomes
easier because the future looks clearer

No more distorted vision because of an illusion
called friendship void of respect

True friendship is dependent upon that quality;
unfortunately, many have died from neglect.

When We Speak A Kind Word

When we speak a kind word, it means a kind word
has been spoken

Words that are heaven sent gives strength to a soul
that may be broken

I'm not a demolition man; Instead, I'd say I'm a
construction worker

I fill blank pages with words to help a tired man go
a little further

I plant the seeds of positivity to strangle the weeds
of the negative

I was blessed with a gift to write, so positive is what
I choose to give.

Whewwwwww, Some People!!!!!!

Some people think they know you though they've
never even met you

Some people want to be loved and cared for but
then won't let you

Some people continuously lie to those they love for
absolutely no reason at all

Some people are really in shock when the stock
others put in them begin to fall

Some people make decisions without considering
the feelings of everyone effected

Some people know exactly what the end will be but
when it comes, they act like it wasn't expected.

Why Is That?

Faith can't be seen, nor can it be heard

It comes from within; it cannot be explained with
words

So when I say, "I believe in a higher power", can
anyone really understand?
If they did, then they would know why I choose
to not believe in man?

Jesus died for us all, yet many of us don't know
how to live
He gave the ultimate gift; yet when when we see
someone in need, we think twice before we give

Unfortunately, what you have just read is a sad
but true fact

The only question I have is, "why is that?"

Wicked People

It's a fact that wicked people often time do wicked deeds

Those people will always have crap happen to them because of the lives they lead

Those people are sometimes able to pull the wool over another wicked persons eyes

Because I can see certain things coming, I really don't understand why they'll act surprised

I mean some things are beyond what I consider to be obvious; They should know better

That's why when the storm of crap starts to fall, they'll be the ones getting wetter

Because they didn't put out positive energy, that umbrella called positive karma will not shield them at all

They'll have to stand in the midst of the storm of crap and wonder what led to their fall.

It's called: You get what you give. PERIOD!!!

Wisdom Acquired

Wisdom is acquired if we learn from life's
experiences and listen to our elders when they speak

If we do both, then it is inevitable that we'll
ultimately gain the knowledge we should all seek

But often times many of us seem to think we know
everything, which would mean there's nothing left
to learn

That's the only way I can explain the look of shock,
disbelief and concern when those type of people get
burned.

Wisdom Is Gained

Wisdom is gained when obstacles and challenges
are introduced to us in some shape or form

This world can be a cold place at times so I treat
wisdom as if it's heat; I use it to keep me warm

Whether it's through my own personal experience or
the experience of another

I can handle any type of climate and remain a
sincerely positive brother

Yes, in the toughest storms I will be the one with
the umbrella of encouragement as I try to shield
some from the elements

Though I must admit, the words that are heard are
really heaven sent.

Words We Choose To Say

A helping hand not only helps one but instead helps two

So always try to help another when the opportunity presents itself to you

Because when you give assistance to a person in need

It shows that you know life is a bed of roses that is fertilized with the caring seed

So be sure to sincerely tell someone to "have a nice day"

Remember, a good deed can begin with the words we choose to say.

Words........

Words can often heal but they too can sometimes hurt

The wrong words can destroy a friendship and all that it's worth

So if you have a relationship that you consider priceless and that you don't want to lose

Thinking twice would be right before deleting; and be extra careful with words you choose to use

I think, speak and subsequently write from experience; so I ask that all please take heed

Some people like "food for thought", and so it's those inquiring minds I intend to feed

With positive blessings in the form of simple, yet real message that should be heard

So that we all have good intentions with words that are mentioned when we feel the need to be heard.

Worthless Perceptions

When we truly believe in ourselves and are happy with who we are and will ultimately become, the perceptions and opinions others have about us really has absolutely no value.........That means their negative thoughts as it pertains to us is actually WORTHLESS!!!!!!!!

We Would've, Could've, Should've…..

Whenever we say, "we could've, we would've or we should've", it is just an opinion or a thought. At some point in our lives, we have all started a sentence with any of those words. When we do, it is a clear indication of one definite fact…………We didn't!!!

You Can Tell..........

You can tell when people haven't bothered to treat
you the way they would want to be treated if they
were in your shoes

There will be a look of disdain which covers
definite pain when they realize its a good
relationship they will ultimately lose

Whether it's a romantic relationship or a working
relationship, a good one is really hard to find

Which is why I am baffled when some people fail to
treat others as equals; perhaps they worship the
devils signs

That's why when some people resort to what I
consider to be bullying tactics

I feel the need to be blunt and up front while telling
them this brother really ain't having it

Don't get it twisted, my words can be an open
helping hand or one that's closed fisted

I will defend myself if disrespect is felt or I can flip
the script and say things that uplift

It is best to understand and accept the fact that we
all get whatever we choose to give

Which means if we are going to work or play together, our ability to coexist peacefully depends on how we live.

Words
Of
Wisdom
Are
Words
To
Live
By

Published by Emerson Welch, Jr

Cover design by Emerson Welch, Jr

ISBN # 978-0-9704569-4-6

www.ingramcontent.com/pod-product-compliance
Lightning Source LLC
Chambersburg PA
CBHW060504030426
42337CB00015B/1734